FUNGI ARE NOT PLANTS

Biology Book Grade 4
Children's Biology Books

BABY PROFESSOR

EDUCATION KIDS

Speedy Publishing LLC

40 E. Main St. #1156

Newark, DE 19711

www.speedypublishing.com

In this book, we're going to cover what fungi are and why they aren't plants. So let's get right to it!

Fungi

HOW ARE FUNGI DIFFERENT FROM PLANTS?

They're growing in your yard, so they must be plants, right? No, that's not true. Originally, scientists believed that fungi were plants or at least related to plants. However, as more data has been gathered, scientists now know that fungi are actually closer to animals than plants, despite the fact that they certainly look more like plants than animals.

There are six kingdoms of classification for all the creatures and plants on Earth. Scientists have determined that fungi don't belong to the animal, plant, or bacteria kingdoms. They have been classified into their own kingdom, simply called fungi.

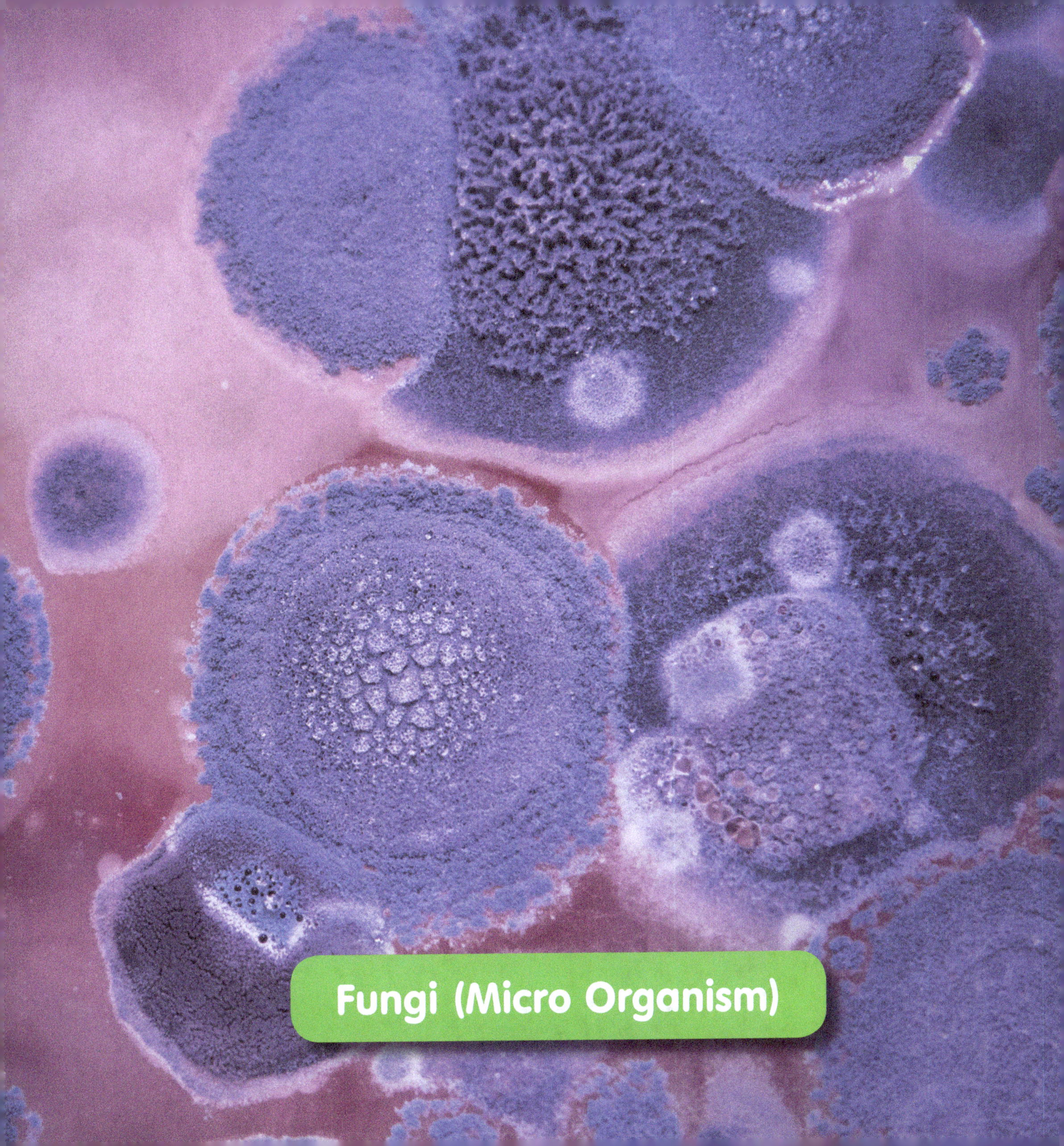

Fungi (Micro Organism)

Molds

THE TWO MAIN CATEGORIES OF CELLS

One of the clues that molds and other type of fungi are not related to bacteria has to do with their cell structure.

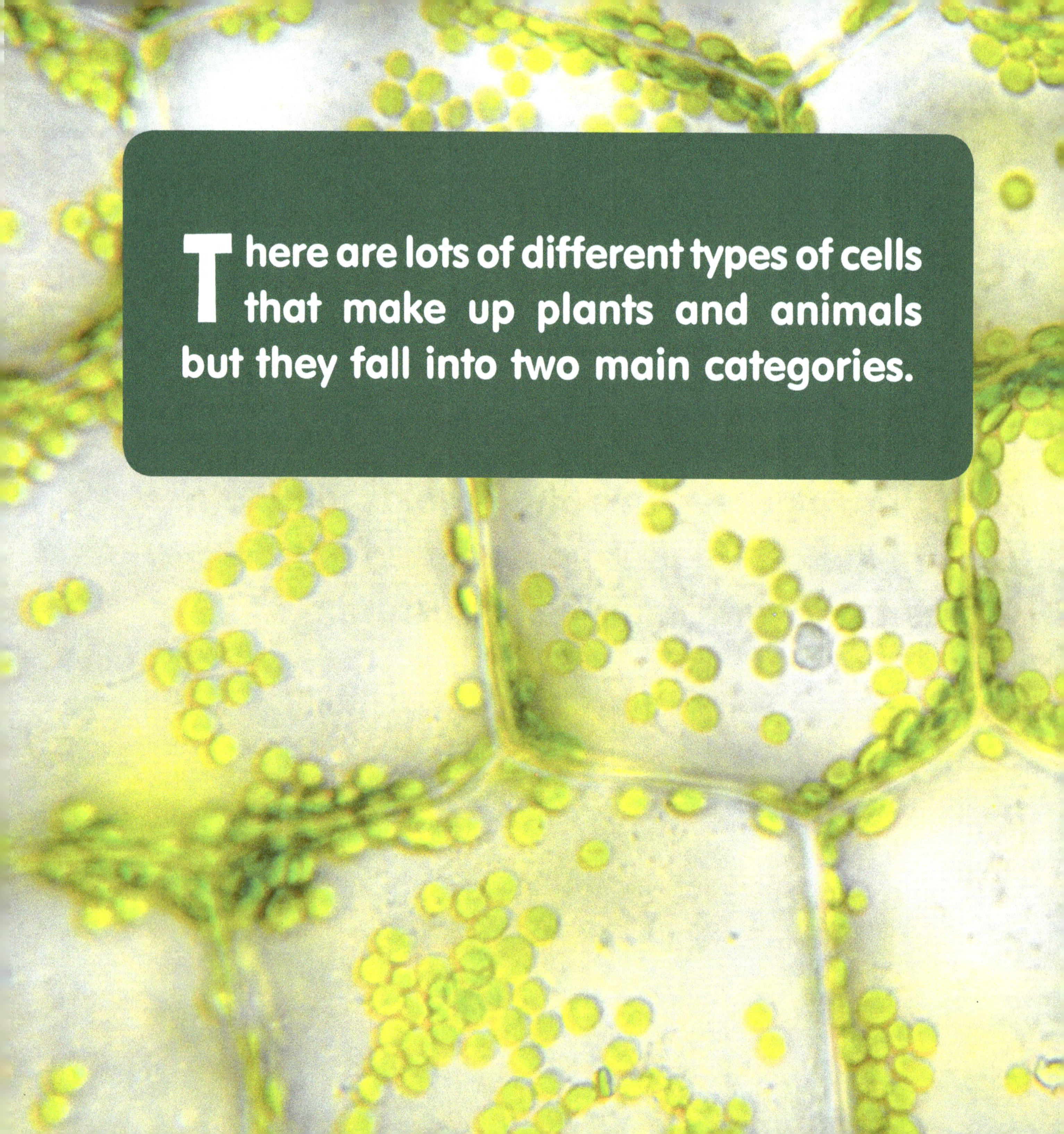

There are lots of different types of cells that make up plants and animals but they fall into two main categories.

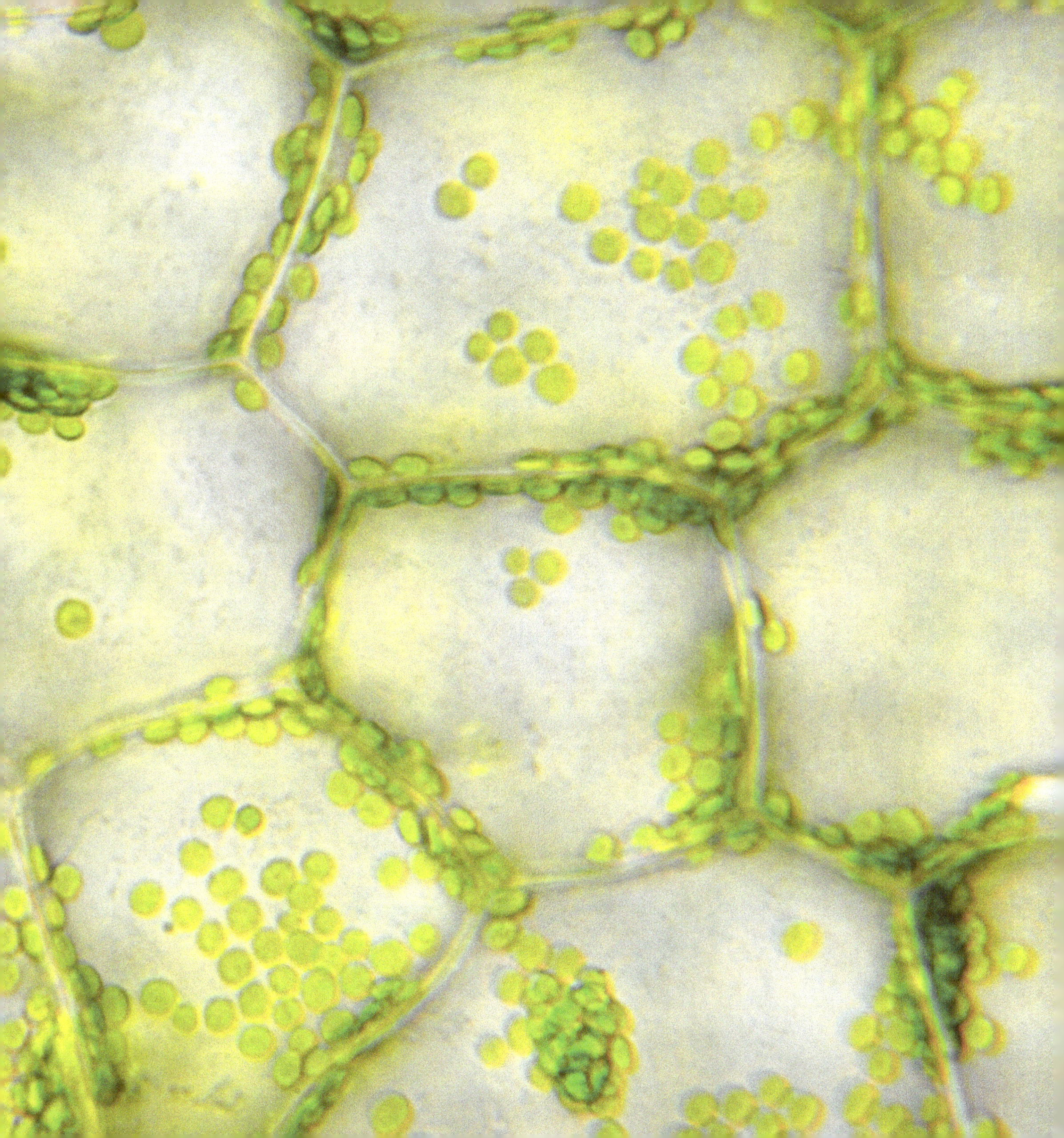

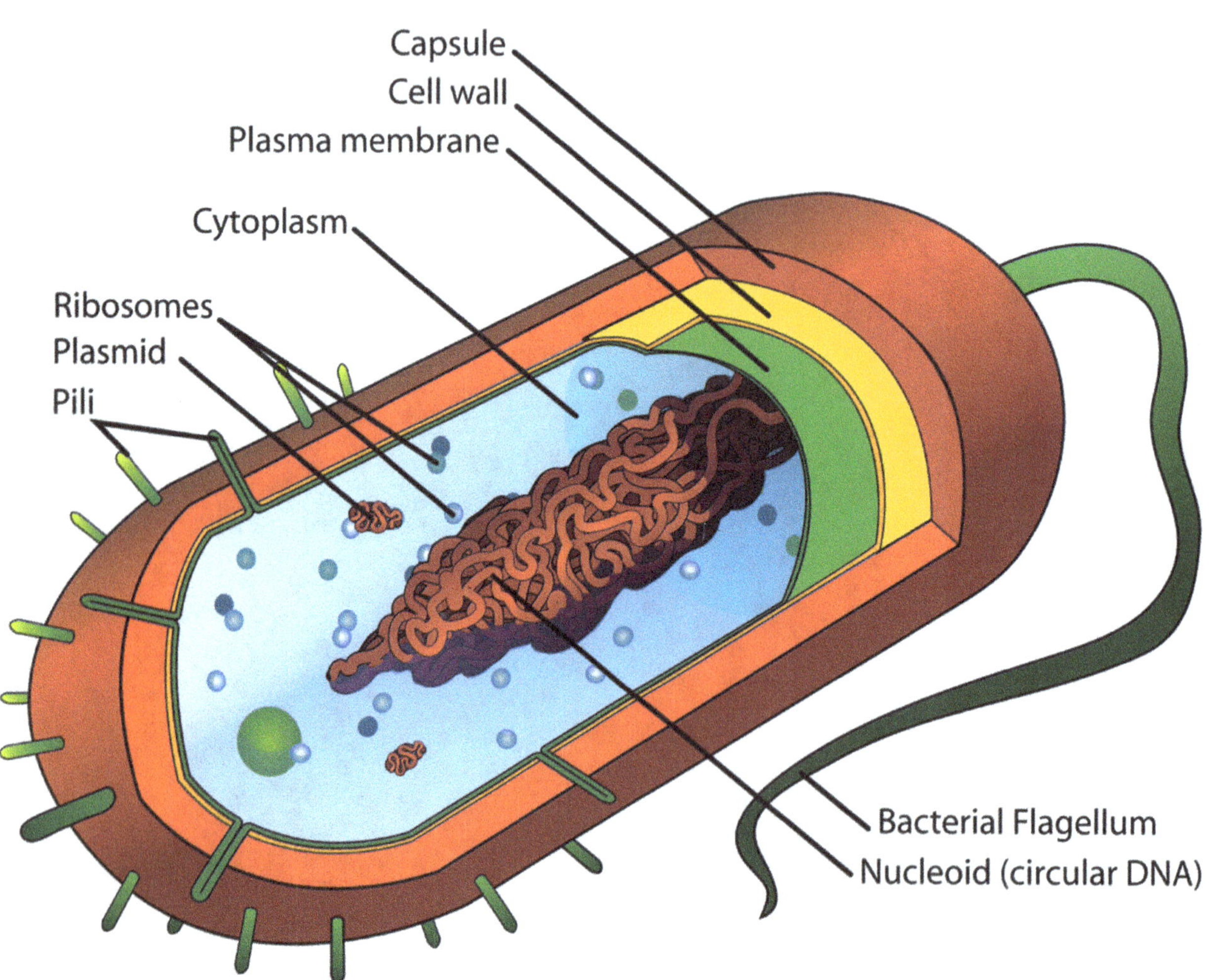

Prokaryotic Cell

A simple cell that doesn't have a nucleus to instruct it what to do is called a prokaryotic cell. Bacteria have these types of cells.

The other main type of cell is a lot larger and quite a bit more complicated than a prokaryotic cell. It's called a eukaryote cell and it has lots of different parts compared to the elementary type of prokaryotic cell.

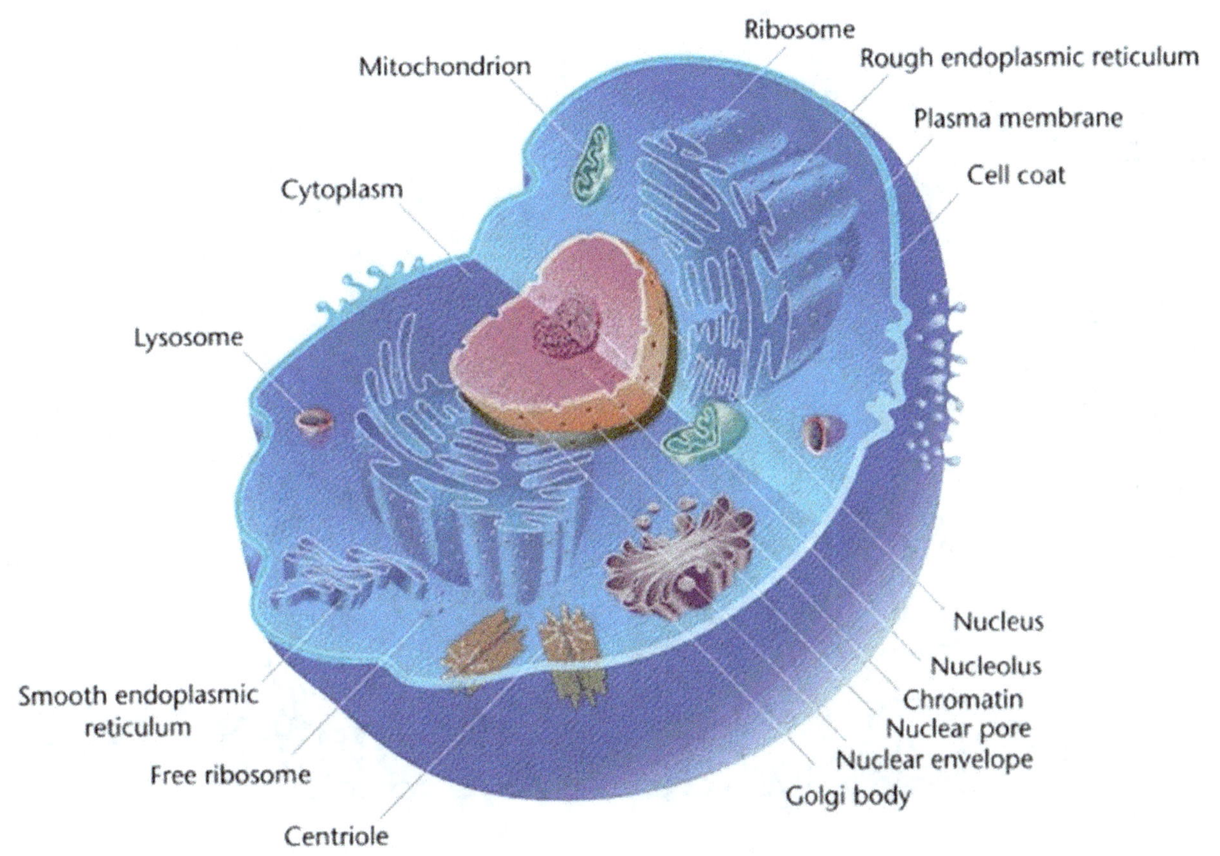

Eukaryotic Cell

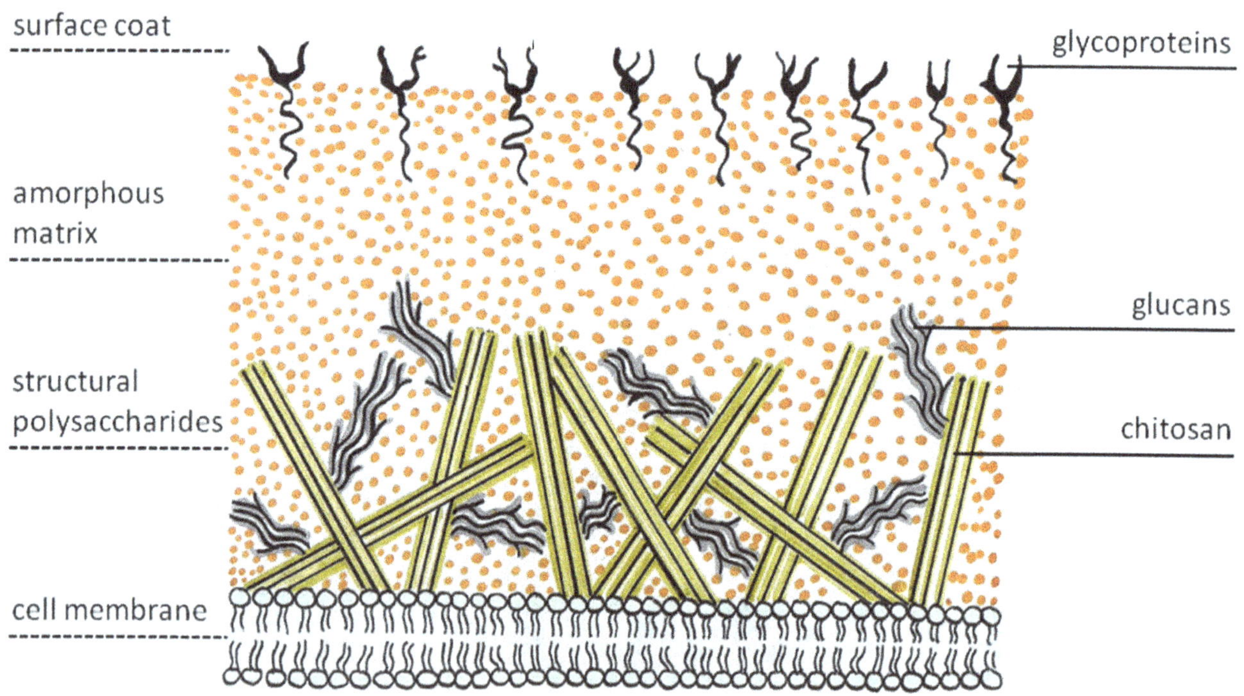

Cell Wall of Fungi

FUNGI ARE NOT PLANTS

Fungi have eukaryote cells like animals and plants do instead of the prokaryotic cells that bacteria have. Because of that, they're not related to bacteria. Even though their cell structure is similar to plants they're not plants because they differ from plants in two very important ways. The cells walls of fungi are made of chitin while the cell walls of plants are made of cellulose.

Chitin is a type of fibrous substance that forms the exoskeletons of certain animals. For example, the exoskeleton of a crab is made of chitin. In this way, fungi more closely resemble animals than plants.

The other major difference is that unlike plants they don't make their own food. Plants make their own food using a process called photosynthesis.

For a long time, scientists classified fungi with the lower plants. These were plants such as mosses, ferns, and also liverworts. Fungi have been classified in their own kingdom since 1969. Recently, scientists have compared their DNA sequences as well as their cell structure to plants and animals. Even though fungi in some cases grow out of the ground and don't move, they're actually more similar to animals than plants. So, when you see a mushroom growing in your backyard, remember it's a type of fungus, not a plant!

Fungus

Fungus in a tree stump

CHARACTERISTICS OF FUNGI

If you were a scientist trying to identify whether a sample could be classified as a fungus, you would consider the following characteristics:

- ➲ Fungi have eukaryotic cells instead of prokaryotic cells.

- ➲ Fungi get their food one of two ways. They consume decomposing matter or they are parasites and eat the bodies of their hosts, which can be either plants or animals.

- They don't have any chlorophyll cells and that means they don't make their own food by photosynthesis.

- They don't reproduce using pollen, seeds, or fruit like plants do. Instead, they reproduce through a large amount of spores.

- Similar to plants, they can't usually move by their own power.

Fungi on a Cabbage Palm

Club Fungi

HOW MANY TYPES OF FUNGI ARE THERE?

There are four major groups of fungi. One of the types is called club fungi. The name comes from the fact that its spores can be found on club-like structures. Shiitake mushrooms are one of the many types of club fungi. Another type is molds. If you've ever seen a damp wall with black mold, this is an example of fungi that falls in the mold group.

The third group of fungi is sac fungi. These fungi produce their reproductive spores in sacs. The yeast that bakers use to make bread rise properly is an example of a sac fungi. The last group of four is the imperfect fungi group. If you've ever had athlete's foot, then you've seen an example of an imperfect fungi.

Sac Fungi

Mushroom

Scientists have identified over 75,000 species of fungi and they believe that there may be as many as a million species that are not yet identified! Separate species are not easy to identify since they frequently look very similar. Scientists who study fungi are called mycologists and they have to use DNA testing to tell the different species apart.

Mushrooms are a common type of fungi. We eat mushrooms but many different types are poisonous. You should never pull a mushroom out of the ground and eat it because it could be deadly poisonous.

Other types of fungi besides mushrooms include all types of molds, the yeast that's used in baking, toadstools and some organisms that are microscopic. Both mushrooms and toadstools are the fruiting bodies of fungi.

A lot more of the organism is found under the ground. The word "fungus" actually comes from the Latin word for mushroom, although there are many other types of fungi besides mushrooms.

Fungi vary greatly in size. They range from microscopic in size to some of the largest living structures on Earth. A honey fungus that measures almost 2.5 miles across that lives in Oregon's Blue Mountains is one of the largest living organisms on the face of the planet!

Honey Fungi

Honey Fungi

Biologists are still debating whether such a structure is a group of organisms or one organism. But most of them believe it's one fungus, singular, instead of a group of fungi, because its cells are all identical and these cells can organize themselves as well as communicate.

Fungi

Fungi thrive and reproduce in damp areas that are dark. Some of their favorite areas to grow are on the bark of mossy trees, on the damp soil near the roots of plants, on warm, wet animals, and even on our skin!

HOW DO FUNGI GET FOOD?

Fungi have two strategies for eating. They either live in or on their food. In order for human beings to eat food, we have enzymes on the inside of our stomachs that break down food so we can process it.

Fungi have the enzymes to break down foods on the outside of their bodies. As they release these enzymes from their bodies, the enzymes break down the nutrients in the host's body into smaller and smaller pieces that they can take in for their food.

For example, think about how a piece of fruit looks when it gets moldy. Mold spores in the air get into food that's left out and then they multiply causing the fruit to decompose.

White Mushroom

WHY ARE FUNGI IMPORTANT?

Fungi are very important in the world's food chain. We wouldn't have many types of bread products without the use of yeast. Yeast is a very simple type of fungi that are round and single celled. There are also many different types of edible mushrooms that both animals and humans eat.

Fungi also play a very important part in decomposition. They break down dead organic matter and while they are using that matter for their own nutrients, they release carbon, oxygen, and nitrogen into the soil and the air.

Some types of fungi are very important in medicines used to heal people. Antibiotics that kill bacterial infections, such as penicillin, are made from fungi.

Jelly Baby Fungi

STRUCTURE OF A FUNGUS

Some fungi are single cells. Yeast falls into this category. However, most are made up of large masses of filaments. These tiny filaments change during the reproductive process. Portions of them transform to make what is called fruiting bodies.

Toadstool

That's why one day you don't see anything in the backyard and then the next day, there are fruiting bodies in the form of mushrooms or toadstools all around. Other types of fruiting bodies are made by fungi too.

HOW DO FUNGI REPRODUCE?

Animals reproduce by laying eggs or by giving live birth. Plants reproduce by spreading their seeds through the wind and pollinators, such as bees or birds. Fungi have unusual ways to reproduce.

Clavarioid Fungi

Bleeding Tooth Fungus

They clone themselves or their spores find each other and join together. However, fungi don't have just male and female types. Instead, they have what scientists call "mating types." There are as many as 20,000 of these different mating types. Scientists have found that filaments from two different organisms can merge their DNA together. No animal or plant species is able to do this.

WHERE DO FUNGI LIVE?

Fungi have been on Earth for over one billion years. They live in the cold, harsh climate of Antarctica, the hot, sultry Amazon jungle, and the dry Gobi desert. They have adapted to every environment and condition on Earth. They even live all over and inside you.

Fungus in Amazon Jungle

Fungi in a tree bark

Awesome! Now you know why fungi are not plants and why they are more closely related to animals. You can find more books about Biology from Baby Professor by searching the website of your favorite book retailer.

Visit

BABY PROFESSOR
EDUCATION KIDS

www.BabyProfessorBooks.com

to download Free Baby Professor eBooks
and view our catalog of new and exciting
Children's Books